IMAGES OF WAR
NAZI CONCENTRATION CAMP OVERSEERS
SONDERKOMMANDOS, KAPOS AND TRAWNIKI MEN

RARE PHOTOGRAPHS FROM WARTIME ARCHIVES

Ian Baxter

Pen & Sword
MILITARY

First published in Great Britain in 2021 by
PEN & SWORD MILITARY
an imprint of
Pen & Sword Books Ltd
47 Church Street
Barnsley
South Yorkshire
S70 2AS

Copyright © Ian Baxter, 2021

ISBN 978-1-52679-995-1

The right of Ian Baxter to be identified as author of this work has been asserted by him in accordance with the Copyright, Designs and Patents Act 1988.

A CIP catalogue record for this book is available from the British Library.

All rights reserved. No part of this book may be reproduced or transmitted in any form or by any means, electronic or mechanical including photocopying, recording or by any information storage and retrieval system, without permission from the Publisher in writing.

Typeset by Concept, Huddersfield, West Yorkshire HD4 5JL
Printed and bound in England by CPI Group (UK) Ltd, Croydon CR0 4YY

Pen & Sword Books Limited incorporates the imprints of Atlas, Archaeology, Aviation, Discovery, Family History, Fiction, History, Maritime, Military, Military Classics, Politics, Select, Transport, True Crime, Air World, Frontline Publishing, Leo Cooper, Remember When, Seaforth Publishing, The Praetorian Press, Wharncliffe Local History, Wharncliffe Transport, Wharncliffe True Crime and White Owl.

For a complete list of Pen & Sword titles please contact
PEN & SWORD BOOKS LIMITED
47 Church Street, Barnsley, South Yorkshire S70 2AS, England
E-mail: enquiries@pen-and-sword.co.uk
Website: www.pen-and-sword.co.uk

Contents

Chapter One
Prelude to Genocide 5

Chapter Two
Sonderkommandos 27

Chapter Three
Kapos 47

Chapter Four
Trawniki Men 63

Chapter Five
Last Years 89

The views or opinions expressed in this book and the context in which the images are used do not necessarily reflect the views or policy of, nor imply approval or endorsement by, the United States Holocaust Memorial Museum (USHMM)

About the Author

Ian Baxter is a military historian who specialises in German twentieth-century military history. He has written more than fifty books including *Poland – The Eighteen Day Victory March*, *Panzers In North Africa*, *The Ardennes Offensive*, *The Western Campaign*, *The 12th SS Panzer-Division Hitlerjugend*, *The Waffen-SS on the Western Front*, *The Waffen-SS on the Eastern Front*, *The Red Army at Stalingrad*, *Elite German Forces of World War II*, *Armoured Warfare*, *German Tanks of War*, *Blitzkrieg*, *Panzer-Divisions at War*, *Hitler's Panzers*, *German Armoured Vehicles of World War Two*, *Last Two Years of the Waffen-SS at War*, *German Soldier Uniforms and Insignia*, *German Guns of the Third Reich*, *Defeat to Retreat: The Last Years of the German Army At War 1943–45*, *Operation Bagration – the Destruction of Army Group Centre*, *German Guns of the Third Reich*, *Rommel and the Afrika Korps*, *U-Boat War*, and most recently *The Sixth Army and the Road to Stalingrad*. He has written over a hundred articles including 'Last days of Hitler', 'Wolf's Lair', 'The Story of the V1 and V2 Rocket Programme', 'Secret Aircraft of World War Two', 'Rommel at Tobruk', 'Hitler's War With his Generals', 'Secret British Plans to Assassinate Hitler', 'The SS at Arnhem', 'Hitlerjugend', 'Battle of Caen 1944', 'Gebirgsjäger at War', 'Panzer Crews', 'Hitlerjugend Guerrillas', 'Last Battles in the East', 'The Battle of Berlin', and many more. He has also reviewed numerous military studies for publication, supplied thousands of photographs and important documents to various publishers and film production companies worldwide, and lectures to various schools, colleges and universities throughout the United Kingdom and the Republic of Ireland.

Chapter One

Prelude to Genocide

It was as far back as March 1933 that the first concentration camp was built by the Nazis, called Dachau. The camp was a far cry from what later characterised the death camps, but even from the beginning its commandant, SS-Brigadeführer Theodor Eicke, was determined to bring hatred and brutality to its inmates. Eicke was the architect, builder, and director of the concentration camp system and looked upon Dachau as a prototype for the concentration camps that followed. Its organisation, layout and construction were developed and ordered by Eicke.

To staff the camps Eicke requested a permanent unit that would be subordinate only to him: the SS-Wachverbände (SS guard groups) were formed. The Wachverbände were independent units within the SS, with their own ranks and command structure. The guards were required to follow Eicke's demands with blind obedience.

By August 1937 the Dachau, Sachsenhausen, Buchenwald and Ravensbrück camps were operating in Germany. The next year, following the Anschluss, Eicke oversaw the building of Mauthausen in Austria.

Each camp was commanded by a Kommandant, who ran the camp with the aid of an adjutant and his command staff. Supervision of the inmates was the responsibility of the Rapportführer, who supervised the daily roll call and daily schedule. The prisoner barracks were operated by a Blockführer, who had one to two squads of SS soldiers to watch over the prisoners.

A period of unrestrained terror followed the invasion of Poland, particularly in what were known as the incorporated territories of Lublin and parts of the provinces of Warsaw and Krakow. In 1940 this area became known as the 'General Government'. It was the dumping ground for all undesirables and enemies of the state. The German authorities established camps in Poland where these undesirables could be incarcerated. It was envisaged that these Poles would be a slave labour force.

Further concentration camps were erected, such as Auschwitz-Birkenau and appeals were made for staff.

These helpers – Hiwis (an abbreviation of Hilfswilliger, volunteer) were far more numerous than the SS personnel. They mainly consisted of Sonderkommandos (special units), Kapos (prisoner functionaries) and Trawniki men (prisoners from East and Central European countries recruited to work for the SS).

A portrait photograph of SS-Obergruppenführer Theodor Eicke. Eicke had been made commandant of Dachau concentration camp in June 1933, and became a major figure in the SS. He was regarded the architect, builder, and director of the concentration camp system and ruled it with an iron fist. It was Eicke that introduced the infamous blue and white striped pyjamas that the inmates wore which came to symbolize the Nazi concentration camps across Europe. While it was Himmler who was ultimately in charge of the concentration camp system, it was Eicke who was the driving force inside the camps.

Aerial view of the Dachau concentration camp. Dachau was located on the grounds of an abandoned munitions factory near the medieval town of Dachau, 10 miles north-west of Munich. It was the first regular concentration camp established by the Nazis and was regarded by Himmler as the first camp for political opponents who were seen as an imminent threat to the new German government. Dachau was established on 20 March 1933. It served as a prototype for the concentration camps that followed. Its basic organisation, layout and construction were developed and ordered by SS-Obergruppenführer Theodor Eicke. *(USHMM, Ray Schmidt)*

(**Above**) View of a wall and guard tower at Dachau. Life for the prisoners inside Dachau was brutal. The SS guards followed Eicke with blind obedience. By drilling his SS guards to hate the prisoners, they were able to mete out severe punishments. *(USHMM, William and Dorothy McLaughlin)*

(**Opposite, above**) Group portrait of SS personnel in the Buchenwald concentration camp. Buchenwald was established in July 1937. It was one of the first and the largest of the concentration camps built in Germany. Many actual or suspected communists were the first to be imprisoned there. *(USHMM, Robert A. Schmuhl)*

(**Opposite, below**) High ranking SS officials on an inspection tour of the Mauthausen concentration camp. Pictured in the front row from left to right are Ernst Kaltenbrunner, Franz Ziereis, Heinrich Himmler, Karl Chmielewski, and August Eigruber. At the far right in the second row is George Bachmayer. The Mauthausen main camp operated from the time of the Anschluss, when Austria was united with the Reich on 8 August 1938. Mauthausen and its subcamps soon become one of the largest labour camp complexes in the concentration camp system. *(USHMM)*

An SS guard supervises work in the Lípa farm labour camp. Lípa, or Umschulungslager Linden bei Deutsch-Brod, was established in Havlickuv Brod in 1940 by the Zentralstelle für Jüdische Auswanderung (Central Office for Jewish Emigration), an authority coordinating all activities associated with Jews after the Protectorate of Bohemia and Moravia had been constituted in March 1939. Lípa camp was designated as a retraining facility. According to Nazi propaganda, Jews were retrained there for working in agriculture before moving to Palestine. *(USHMM, Oldrich Stransky)*

SS officers bid farewell to SS platoon squad commander Schramm at Gross-Rosen. Anton Thumann is pictured fifth from the left. Artur Roedl is in the front centre. Kuno Schramm is in the first row, far right. Dr Friedrich Entress is probably standing third from the left. Gross-Rosen concentration camp was erected in the summer of 1940 as a satellite camp of Sachsenhausen. Initially slave labour was carried out in a huge stone quarry owned by the SS-Deutsche Erd- und Steinwerke GmbH (SS German Earth and Stone Works). *(USHMM, Martin Mansson)*

(**Above**) Close-up portrait of three SS officers in Gross-Rosen concentration camp. Pictured on the far right is the adjutant, Kuno Schramm. By May 1941, Gross-Rosen became an independent camp, and as the complex grew most prisoners were put to work in the new Nazi enterprises attached to the sub-camps. *(USHMM, Martin Mansson)*

(**Opposite, above**) Commandant Franz Ziereis poses with members of the SS staff of the Mauthausen concentration camp. From left to right are Haupsturmführer Erich Wasitzky (apothecary); Karl Schulz, chief of the Politischer Abteilung (the Gestapo office in the camp); Ziereis (camp commandant); Sturmbannführer Eduard Krebsbach (doctor); Karl Boehmichen (doctor) and an unidentified Obersturmführer. *(USHMM, Eugene S. Cohen)*

(**Opposite, below**) Sachsenhausen prisoners, wearing uniforms with triangular badges, stand in columns under the supervision of a camp guard. *(NARA)*

(**Opposite, above**) A group portrait of SS officers in front of a barrack in the Hinzert concentration camp. Pictured on the far right is Anton Ganz. Hinzert camp held mainly political prisoners from all ages. Many were in transit towards larger concentration camps where most would be killed. However, a significant number of prisoners were murdered at Hinzert. (*USHMM, Robert A. Schmuhl*)

(**Opposite, below**) A group of SS officers are viewing something on the ground in the Buchenwald concentration camp. (*USHMM, Robert A. Schmuhl*)

(**Above**) SS officers supervising the construction of a gallows in the forest near Buchenwald concentration camp. (*USHMM, Robert A. Schmuhl*)

A member of the German SS supervises the boarding of Jews onto trains during a deportation action in the Krakow ghetto. This deportation of Jews is more than likely going to Auschwitz. *(USHMM)*

Jews from the Lodz ghetto board trains for the Chełmno death camp. The deportees both arrived and departed by train at the Radogoszcz railway station in Marysin, and proceeded on foot in columns to or from the ghetto. *(USHMM)*

Jewish men and women prepare to sort clothing confiscated from the deportees to Chełmno. The camp was established specially to carry out mass killings. It operated from 8 December 1941 to 11 April 1943, and operations were run alongside Belzec, Sobibor and Treblinka extermination camps. (*USHMM, Sidney Harcsztark*)

A young Jewish woman writes her last letter before boarding the deportation train on the journey to Chełmno. (*USHMM, Leopold Page Photographic Collection*)

(**Opposite, above**) A Policeman oversees a deportation action of Jews on what appears to be open-topped freight cars. In early 1942, the SS and police began deportations from the Lodz Ghetto to the Chełmno death camp. German officials transported the Jews from Łódź by train to Koło railway station, 6 miles north-west of Chełmno. From there the SS and police personnel supervised transfer of the Jews from the freight as well as passenger trains to smaller-size cargo trains, as shown in this photograph, running on a narrow-gauge track, which took them from Koło to the Powiercie station. Note the child nearest to the camera pointing to a family member directing him to a space on the train.

(**Opposite, below**) German police round-up Jews and load them onto trucks in the Ciechanow Ghetto.
(*USHMM, Instytut Pamieci Narodowej*)

(**Above**) Jews preparing to board a train destined for Treblinka death camp. On 22 July 1942 SS personnel received a telegram to say that the first trains would start travelling between Warsaw and Treblinka. It confirmed that the trains would have sixty closed cars each, and that they would be transporting deportees from the Warsaw ghetto. They would be unloaded and then sent back empty.

(**Opposite, above**) SS guards stand in formation outside the commandant's house near Belzec concentration camp. Pictured (in the front row from right to left) are Heinrich Barbl and SS-Oberwachtmeister Artur Dachsel; (second row) SS-Hauptscharführer Lorenz Hackenholt, SS-Unterscharführer Ernst Zierke, SS-Untersturmführer Karl Gringers (front), and SS-Untersturmführer Fritz Tauscher (second from the left).

(**Opposite, below**) A group of SS officers gather together [probably in Dachau]. Pictured on the far right is Martin Gottfried Weiss. Richard Gluecks is in the centre facing to the right. Martin Gottfried Weiss served as Commandant of Neuengamme, Dachau and Majdanek concentration camps. An SS-Obersturmbannführer he eventually was promoted to Inspector of the Concentration Camps. (*USHMM, Joseph Crane*)

(**Above**) Crematoria in Majdanek death camp. The camp had seven gas chambers, two wooden gallows, some 227 structures in all, placing it among the largest of Nazi-run concentration camps. (*USHMM, Panstwowe Muzeum na Majdanku*)

A warehouse filled with containers of the deadly chemical Zyklon B (poison gas pellets) at the Majdanek death camp. (*USHMM, Instytut Pamieci Narodowej*)

The crematoria in Dachau. The camp staff were mostly of SS men, although nineteen female guards eventually served at Dachau. A number of Norwegians worked as guards along with Kapos and Sonderkommandos. (*NARA*)

Jewish police were recruited to relieve the SS and other personnel of camp tasks. This photograph was taken in the Westerbork transit camp where police stand in formation during a roll call. The Jewish police in Westerbork were universally detested by camp inmates for their cruelty and for their collaboration with the Nazis. Composed primarily of Dutch and German Jews, the OD was responsible for guarding the punishment block, organizing transports and maintaining order in the camp. The police force consisted of 20 men in mid-1942, growing to 182 in April 1943. They wore the 'OD' badge on the left breast as decreed in camp order no. 27 of 23 April 1943. (*USHMM, Trudi Gidan*)

(**Above**) Members of the Ordendienst (Jewish police) supervise the deportation of Jews from the Westerbork transit camp. The Ordendienst did not usually have official uniforms, often wearing just an identifying armband or hat, and a badge. They were not allowed to carry firearms, but they did carry truncheons or whips. (*USHMM, Trudi Gidan*)

(**Opposite, above**) Members of the Ordendienst give assistance to prisoners boarding a deportation train in the Westerbork transit camp. Westerbork was a transit camp for Jews who were being deported from the Netherlands to killing centres in Poland. The camp was initially established in October 1939 by the Dutch government to house Jewish refugees who had entered the country illegally. It was constructed on a tract of heath and marshland on the outskirts of the village of Westerbork in the province of Drenthe. (*USHMM, Trudi Gidan*)

(**Opposite, below**) Jewish police escort a group of women who have been rounded up for deportation in the Lodz ghetto. (*USHMM, Arie Ben Menachem*)

Chapter Two

Sonderkommandos

At the Wannsee conference held in Berlin in January 1942 it was agreed that it would be the Jews in the General Government that would be dealt with first. The Nazi leadership was under no illusion that it would require great organizational skills to deal with the effective means of mass murder. A pool of experts was drafted in to undertake this mammoth task.

It was decided to transport European and other Jews to Poland and to kill them there, and Auschwitz was set up as a vast labour pool and death camp. Other new camps too were ordered to be erected solely for extermination in Poland. Jews would be transported to them mainly using the rail network.

There were, however, massive problems with transportation when the Nazis were still at war, and the concentration camp system would be burdened by the workload of overseeing such a mammoth operation. The problems of adapting the camps into killing centres was equally challenging. There were problems of overcrowding, of endless trainloads of prisoners, there were problems of acquiring materials. The gassings posed a number of problems, including the disposal of corpses.

The Kapos were already overworked by the constant flow of new transports. It was therefore agreed that units of inmates would be selected for duties. The SS called them Sonderkommando (special units) (they were unrelated to the existing military SS-Sonderkommando consisting of German soldiers). The Sonderkommando were almost exclusively Jews.

Only fit men were selected for special duties, and in most cases they were inducted immediately on their arrival at the camp, forced into their role under threat of death. Because the SS needed them to remain physically fit, they were given less squalid living conditions than other inmates. They were given their own barracks and allowed to keep various foods, and other items such as medicine and cigarettes. Unlike ordinary prisoners they were not so often subject to random beatings by guards and Kapos, or so often shot for insubordination. However, their lives depended on how well they worked and how efficiently they would assist in keeping the death camps running smoothly for the SS.

The Sonderkommando were not given any advance warning of the undertakings they had to perform. A duty that they did not have to participate in was killing; that responsibility was retained for the SS. The primary tasks of these special units were to assist in camp duties such as unloading Jews from trains, with the assistance of the order commandos (Aufräumungskommando) who were a group of recruited Jews also used to unload the confiscated property off the transports. With the assistance of the Sonderkommandos, they collected possessions and then sorted them for storage in the warehouse complex known as 'Kanada'. The Sonderkommandos also allocated work details, but this normally came under the supervision of the Kapos.

The Sonderkommandos were required to calm the Jewish arrivals who had been selected for death, and escort them to the gas chambers. After they got them to undress, they would have to wait while they were gassed. After dragging their dead bodies from the gas chamber, they were tasked with crematorium and body disposal duties. Sometimes inductees would find the task psychologically challenging. Some were themselves fathers and had families and were not up to the mental strain, particularly when women and children were involved. Sometimes they discovered members of their own families among the bodies. On occasion there were disputes and refusals to obey orders. However, these special units were not allowed to refuse orders or to resign. If they did not commit suicide, they would be removed by the guards and shot.

The Nazis could not allow the secret of their genocidal activities to get out. The Kapos and Sonderkommandos would never be allowed to escape. They were Geheimnisträger (bearers of secrets) and as such were held in isolation away from prisoners being used as slave labour.

One camp that had a massive pool of Sonderkommando was Auschwitz-Birkenau. In early 1942 Birkenau adapted a building for murder known as the 'little red house', renamed Bunker I. It was first made operational on 20 March. Under the cover of darkness the Jews were transported there.

According to the Kommandant, Rudolf Höss,

> The transport was conducted by Aumeier and Palitzsch and some block leaders. They talked with the Jews about general topics, their qualifications and trades, with a view of misleading them. On arrival at the 'Cottage' they were told to undress. At first they went calmly into the rooms where they were supposed to be disinfected. But some of them showed signs of panic. Immediately all the Jews still outside were pushed into the chambers and the doors screwed shut. At the first signs of unrest, those responsible were unobtrusively led behind the building and killed with a small-calibre gun, which was inaudible to the others. The presence and calm behaviour of the Special Detachment [Sonderkommando] served to reassure those who were worried or who suspected what was about to happen. A further calming effect was obtained by

members of the Special Detachment accompanying them into the rooms and remaining there until the last moment, while an SS-man also stood in the doorway until the end.

Despite the limited panic, the SS confirmed that the first gassing operation in Birkenau had been a complete success. Most of the Jews had calmly filed into the Little Red House with no disturbance to the normal operation of camp life.

Now they had to dispose of the evidence. Before there was a crematorium on site the only solution was to bury the corpses in a nearby pit. This was done by Sonderkommando.

Here is another quotation from Höss about the arrival of Jewish prisoners:

> In front of the farmhouse they all had to undress behind specially erected screens ... On the doors were the inscriptions 'Disinfection Room'. The SS sub-alterns on duty had the order to tell these people, with the help of interpreters, that they should take proper care of their belongings so that they might find them again immediately after de-lousing. These measures were intended to avoid any disquiet.

Very often no incidents occurred,

> It was most important that when they arrived the entire procedure of undressing should take place in an atmosphere of the greatest possible calm. People reluctant to undress were helped by those that had already undressed, or by men of the Sonderkommando.

All through the procedure the victims were told calmly that they were to bathe and be deloused. Once crammed inside the gas chamber and the doors shut SS-Unterscharführer Otto Moll, dressed in a white protective suit with gasmask, threw the saturated Zyklon B pellets through a little vent and then waited twenty-five minutes until the screams of those fighting for their lives fell silent. During the gassing procedure SS surgeons on duty in the camp waited with an SS hospital orderly with oxygen apparatus to revive SS men in case any were affected by the poisonous fumes. Once they were certain that all inside were dead the doors and the windows were opened to ventilate the rooms. The tangled corpses were then removed by the Sonderkommando for disposal.

The Sonderkommando attached leather thongs to the bodies and then pulled them along on a concrete surface, often through shallow water, to a point in front of the furnaces. Usually, before cremation or burial took place, a Sonderkommando known as the 'dentist' inspected the corpses for gold teeth or dentures and then began extracting them with a chisel or hammer. Any gold found in the victim's mouths was placed in a jar containing acid. The 'dentist' was also given the gruesome task of searching other body cavities for smuggled valuables. When he had confirmed that the gassed and now mutilated corpse was 'clean', the body could now be buried. The Sonderkommando would then drag the victims to a wagon, which was sometimes on rails, and transported the murdered victims to a nearby pit. Later, when crematoria had been built, the bodies were placed face up head to foot on a metal 'corpse board' that ran on rollers, which was then pushed into the oven for incineration.

(**Below**) German soldiers oversee the boarding of Jews from the Zyradow ghetto onto a deportation train.
(*USHMM, Instytut Pamieci Narodowej*)

(**Opposite, above**) Jews from the Warsaw ghetto board a deportation train with the assistance of Jewish police.
(*USHMM, Instytut Pamieci Narodowej*)

(**Opposite, below**) Deported Jews being unloading from a train with their belongings. They are being assisted by members of the camp's Sonderkommando wearing their distinctive stripy blue and white clothing and white Sonderkommando armband. The Sonderkommando were almost exclusively Jews.

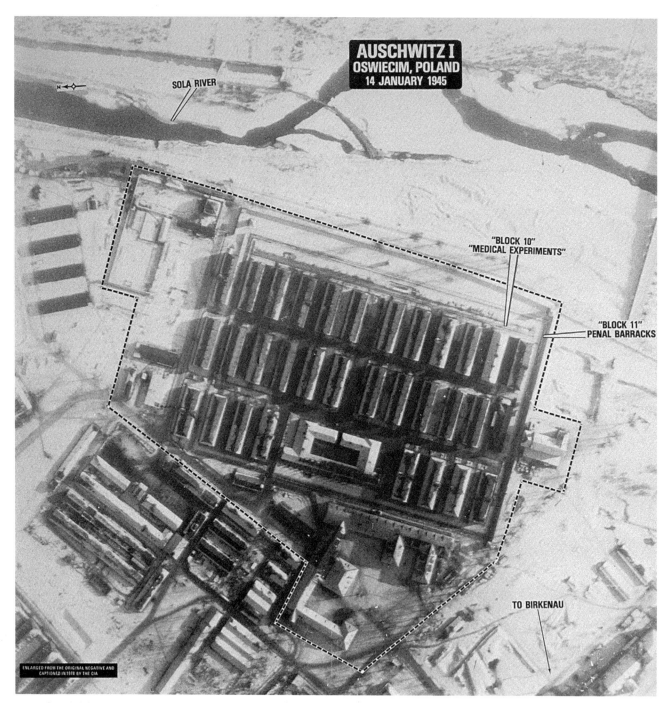

An aerial photograph of Auschwitz I concentration camp. *(NARA)*

An aerial photograph of Auschwitz II (Birkenau). (NARA)

(**Above**) Prisoners in the Aufräumungskommando (cleaning commandos) unload the confiscated property of transport of Jews. The Sonderkommando would sort these possessions in the 'Kanada'. There were Kanada storage facilities in many of the barracks and other buildings around the camp. The looted property was put to various uses in the Third Reich. *(USHMM, Yad Vashem)*

(**Opposite, above**) Officials at the Monowitz-Buna building site greet Himmler and his inspection team. Among those pictured are Max Faust (left, wearing a suit), the manager of building operations for IG Farben in Monowitz-Buna; Ernst Schmauser (shaking hands with Faust), and Himmler (far right). Auschwitz commandant Rudolph Höss is second from the left, next to Faust. Höss recruited hundreds of Sonderkommandos for camp duties. Later, under SS supervision, they ran the gas chambers and crematoria, being known as camp stokers. *(USHMM, Instytut Pamieci Narodowej)*

(**Opposite, below**) A row of ovens in one of the crematoria at Auschwitz. Sonderkommandos were Arbeitshäftlinge, slaves required to operate the death camp.

(**Above**) Jews from Subcarpathian Rus await selection on the ramp at Auschwitz-Birkenau. On the left is a group of uniformed prisoners from the Kanada commando and a few SS men. The Sonderkommandos were here on the ramps assisting in the arrival and helping the Kanada commandos sort the possessions. (*Auschwitz-Birkenau Museum*)

(**Opposite**) Two photographs showing Jews from Subcarpathian Rus undergo selection on the ramp at Auschwitz-Birkenau. Sonderkommandos are unloading the new arrivals from the freight cars. Pictured in front holding a riding crop may be either SS-Unterscharführer Wilhelm Emmerich or SS-Haupsturmführer Georg Hocker, assisted by the Jewish prisoner identified as Hans Schorr. (*Auschwitz-Birkenau Museum*)

A transport of Jews are taken off trains and assembled on the ramp at Auschwitz-Birkenau. They are being assisted by Jewish prisoners, Sonderkommandos and, more than likely, Kanada commandos. Note the chimneys of the crematoria in the far distance. (*Auschwitz-Birkenau Museum*)

Three photographs show Jews from Subcarpathian Rus undergo selection on the ramp at Auschwitz-Birkenau. Again pictured are Emmerich, Hocker, and Hans Schorr. Among the crowd are Jewish prisoners and Sonderkommandos assisting. (*Auschwitz-Birkenau Museum*)

Jews await selection on the ramp at Auschwitz-Birkenau. In the foreground prisoners from the Kanada commando stand near a group of SS men. *(Auschwitz-Birkenau Museum)*

(**Opposite & following page**) Clandestine photos taken in Auschwitz-Birkenau showing members of the Sonderkommando laying gassed corpses in a field and burning them. Open air burning procedures like this was not uncommon at Auschwitz-Birkenau. Due to the high numbers gassed at the camp the crematoria's often exceeded their official incineration capacity, and as a result the crematoria began overflowing with the dead. These two photos are part of a series taken by an inmate called Alex, and it was members of the Sonderkommando in Crematorium V that helped obtain and hide the camera, and acted as lookouts. A Sonderkommando called Fajnzylberg, who had worked at Crematorium V since July 1943, described: 'On the day on which the pictures were taken … we allocated tasks. Some of us were to guard the person taking the pictures. In other words, we were to keep a careful watch for the approach of anyone who did not know the secret, and above all for any SS men moving about in the area. At last the moment came. We all gathered at the western entrance leading from the outside to the gas-chamber of Crematorium V: we could not see any SS men in the watchtower overlooking the door from the barbed wire, nor near the place where the pictures were to be taken. Alex, the Greek Jew, quickly took out his camera, pointed it towards a heap of burning bodies, and pressed the shutter. This is why the photograph shows prisoners from the Sonderkommando working at the heap. One of the SS was standing beside them, but his back was turned towards the crematorium building. Another picture was taken from the other side of the building, where women and men were undressing among the trees. They were from a transport that was to be murdered in the gas-chamber of Crematorium V.'

Crematorium IV, summer 1943. The gas chambers are located in the lower wing (left) of the building. At the end of June 1944, owing to the increased demand on cremations, the Sonderkommando were moved from their barracks to live in Crematoria II, III and IV. (*Auschwitz-Birkenau State Museum*)

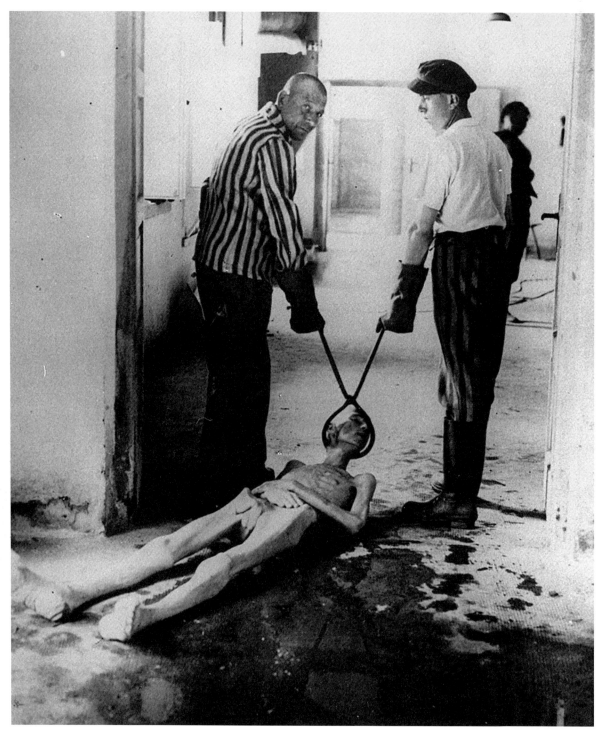

(**Above & Opposite**) Two survivors re-enact how the crematoria ovens operated by the Sonderkommando (probably in Dachau). Once the bodies had been gassed the Sonderkommando attached leather thongs to the bodies and pulled them along the concrete surface into the incinerator room in front of the furnaces. They were then placed face up head to foot on a metal 'corpse board' that ran on rollers and was pushed into the oven. Incineration normally took forty-five minutes to one hour. (*USHMM, Albert Schiff, R. Harrison*)

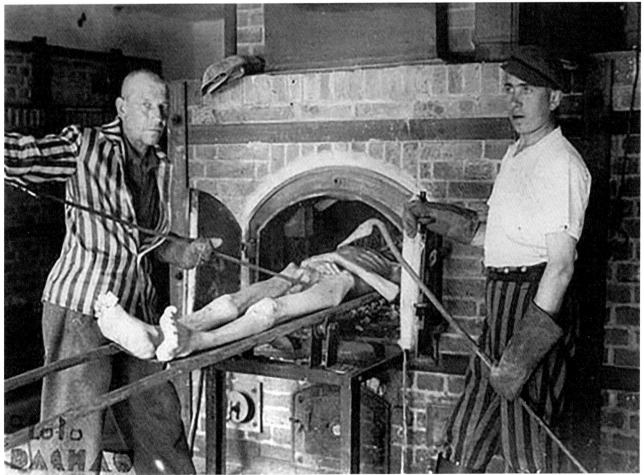

Two survivors re-enact how the crematorium ovens were operated by the Sonderkommando (probably in Dachau). (*USHMM, Ginny Helgeson*)

Chapter Three

Kapos

Due to the implementation of government policies and the increased numbers of inmates into the camps, the SS delegated the workload to selected prisoners. It was agreed to select up to 10 per cent of the inmates of camps for overseer duties.

Initially the SS selected only criminal prisoners as overseers. This had been the policy at both Buchenwald and Mauthausen. They were nicknamed 'Kapos' (camp foreman/comrade police) by the SS, but the official government title for them was prison functionaries or Funktionshäftling.

The Kapos were given a brief training. They were taught the regulations applicable to all concentration camps, 'how to detect sabotage and work slowdowns, how to prevent escapes, and how to punish prisoners within the parameters of camp regulations'. It was emphasized that the Kapos were to have no personal relationship whatsoever with any of the prisoners. Some were sympathetic to the prisoners, but those who deviated from the standard mentality of cruelty were punished.

With their training completed, to distinguish themselves from the prisoners they were assigned a camp policeman/Lagerpolizist armband, worn on the left arm. They were also identified by a green triangle as Berufsverbrecher or BV (career criminal). There were a number of different levels within the Kapo designation: the Lagerältester (camp leader) who served largely in administrative roles. This was the highest prisoner position and came with the most privileges. Then there were the Blockältester (block leaders). They were responsible for the administration and discipline of an entire barracks. They had their own private room (or shared with an assistant) and better rations. Then there was the Stubenälteste (section leader), who oversaw parts of larger barracks and reported to the Blockältester.

The Kapos were rewarded with extra food, cigarettes, alcohol or other privileges, and for their own survival did what was needed to assist the SS.

Kapos were put in charge of the transportation of Jews from the ghettos into the stations and rail sidings where they would be escorted on foot to the selected concentration camp. They would also oversee the unloading of Jews from the cattle cars and support the movement of them following 'ramp' selection: those selected for camp and labour duties and those chosen to be immediately sent to their death.

Other duties were administrative: food and clothing stock control, barrack designation of prisoners, overseeing the removal and stock of personal possessions taken from Jews on their arrival in the camps, roll calls, and overseeing the prisoners during forced labour duties. In fact there was a host of tasks given to the Kapos to relieve the burden on the SS.

Some Kapos were able to secretly help the prisoners with extra food and easier jobs. But some had no scruples and did not hesitate to inflict pain on the prisoners. Some were eager to show their SS superiors that they could be as brutal as them. There were Kapos like Ernst Krankemann at Auschwitz, who would whip and beat the inmates, and went about his daily business in the camp showing no sympathy for them at all.

The first trainload of prisoners assigned to Birkenau consisted of 999 able-bodied Slovakian women Jews. They were greeted by the Kapos as the train steamed its way into Auschwitz station on 26 March 1942. The Jews were unloaded from the ramps just outside the station. For many that disembarked from the crammed cattle cars that day the railway stop was very much like any other provincial railway station. But in fact it was very different. Under supervision of SS guards, local police, and screaming Kapos, they were marched through the town of Auschwitz to the main camp, ordered to run in groups of five. Those unable to run were beaten by Kapos, and if they still did not move, they were simply killed on the spot by the SS, who were always armed.

The Nazis created brothels in a number of camps. The first camp brothel was established in Mauthausen/Gusen in 1942. In 1943 Auschwitz established one, as did Buchenwald. A year later another two were established in Neuengamme and then Dachau. These brothels were supposed to be used as an incentive for prisoners to collaborate, but they were used mostly by Kapos because regular inmates were usually too incapacitated to use them.

(**Opposite**) Two photographs showing the deportation of Jews being escorted by the Jewish Police. The Jewish Police were technically ghetto overseers. They were responsible for a multitude of tasks. Although chiefly raised to assist the German police battalions guarding the ghetto wall and gates, their duties were far greater than that. They were in charge of distributing food rations and welfare duties such as aiding the poor. They collected personal belongings, valuables, and accompanied labour battalions that worked outside the ghetto. They also participated in the round-up of Jews for mass deportations, handing over the deportation tasks to the SS, Trawniki or Kapos. (USHMM, Sidney Harcsztark and Benjamin (Miedzyrzecki) Meed)

A column of prisoners walks from the Buna camp (Auschwitz III–Monowitz) towards the IG Farben works. Behind them is an SS barracks (headquarters, residential barrack for the guards, etc). A guard gave this photograph to Auschwitz survivor Nina Schuldenrein. Kapos would assist in work details, ensuring the labourers were marching quickly enough to their place of work, and then ensure their tasks were carried out properly. (*Auschwitz-Birkenau Museum*)

Jewish work column during the summer of 1941 in the town of Mahilyow. Work details regularly left the camps and worked long hours, undertaking a multitude of tasks, often being starved and beaten.

A Kapo with his armband worn over his coat.

An SS officer can be seen walking towards a Jewish work detail before they commence work. The work force was often supervised by Kapos.

At a labour camp and Jewish inmates can be seen breaking up stones and having them transported on narrow-gauge rail lines. Kapos had been taught how to detect work slowdowns, and were quick to punish prisoners, often severely.

A Jewish work detail moving stones.

Two photographs taken in sequence showing what appears to be a Jewish policeman beating a prisoner and a Kapo who is partially hidden in the photo at the Cieszanów labour camp. *(USHMM, Benjamin (Miedzyrzecki) Meed)*

Jewish prisoners in Płaszów at forced labour. The man at right is a Kapo. (*USHMM, Leopold Page Photographic Collection*)

Prisoners during forced labour appear to be digging a ditch for a drainage system in the Neuengamme concentration camp. Note the Kapo overseeing the work with a truncheon or whip. Neuengamme became the largest concentration camp in north-west Germany with over 100,000 prisoners being sent there during its operational lifetime. (*USHMM, KZ-Gedenkstatte Neuengamme*)

Two photographs in sequence showing Mordechai Chaim Rumkowski, head of the Jewish Council of Elders in the Łódź Ghetto (seated centre) attending an event with Jewish Police, Kapo members and Sonderkommando. Also pictured is Leon Rozenblat, chief of the ghetto police (seated at the right, holding his cap). The man behind Rumkowski may be Stanislaw Jakobson, president of the ghetto court. *(USHMM, Gila Flam)*

Prisoners at forced labour in the Janowska concentration camp. The men are being supervised by Kapos and what appears to be a guard with a whip. *(USHMM, Belarusian State Archive of Documentary Film and Photography)*

Kapos, Jewish Police and a member of the German Police Battalion can be seen standing together with local children following a deportation action of Jews from a ghetto.

A typical Kapo armband worn on the left arm.

A photograph showing what looks like an SS propaganda cameraman depicting the lives of prisoners at a labour camp. To the left of the photo is a Kapo overseeing the work detail.

Jewish prisoners at forced labour in Płaszów. Płaszów concentration camp was divided into male and female prisoners sections, camp personnel, work facilities, and a further subdivision between Jews and non-Jews. There was also a private barracks for the Kapos and their families. While the primary function of the camp was forced labour, it was not an extermination camp and did not have gas chamber or crematorium facilities. Mass shootings were, however, carried out, especially of those unable to work. (USHMM, Leopold Page Photographic Collection)

Jewish prisoners at forced labour in Płaszów. The building on the left is probably the Madritch factory office. The man walking in the foreground is likely a Kapo. (USHMM, Leopold Page Photographic Collection)

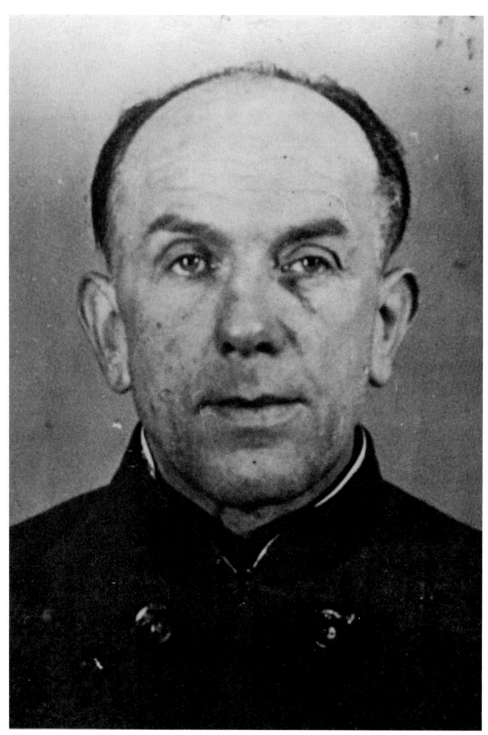

Alfons Wagner, a kapo in Ebensee and Mauthausen 1944-45. *(Yad Vashem)*

Prisoners at a forced labour building the Dove–Elbe canal. The Kapos wear white and black armbands. Pictured at the front left facing the camera and digging with a shovel is Salo Blechner, who survived over five years as a prisoner of several concentration camps, being liberated at Belsen in April 1945. *(USHMM, KZ-Gedenkstatte Neuengamme)*

Chapter Four

Trawniki Men

On 22 June 1941 the German war machine attacked the Soviet Union. Three months later while the Wehrmacht were battling across Russia and the four Einsatzgruppen (action groups) were creating a bloodbath in the rear areas, Russian PoWs were being picked by the SS to volunteer to assist them carry out the Holocaust. The plan was an idea of Himmler's, who had instructed Odilo Globočnik to start recruiting mainly Ukrainian auxiliaries from the Soviet PoWs, due to close relations with the local Ukrainian Hilfsverwaltung (helper auxiliary).

Globočnik chose SS-Hauptsturmführer Karl Streibel to head selection and training and, with the assistance of his new officers, visited all the Russian PoW camps, which mainly contained those captured along the border regions when the Wehrmacht had first launched their invasion, although there were a number of Volksdeutsche from Eastern Europe among them too. Following individual screening, they began recruiting.

They were valuable because many could speak Polish, Russian and Ukrainian. Other nationalities enlisted were Estonians, Latvians, Lithuanians, Armenians, Belarusians, Ukrainians and conscripted civilians.

Between September 1941 and September 1942, the SS drafted some 2,500 men to work for them. By summer 1943 this number had risen to 3,700 and 5,000 by the end of 1944. These Hiwis (willing helpers) would be trained as Wachmänner (guards) at a special camp named Trawniki, which was in the village of that name 18 miles south-east of Lublin. The training facility was adjacent to the Trawniki concentration camp for Jews who had been deported from the Warsaw Ghetto.

At Trawniki, Streibel was appointed leader and trainer of what he termed 'auxiliary police'. They would work in the General Government and assist the SS in genocide.

Streibel favoured the more aggressive and violent recruits. The trainers drilled the volunteers to hate the Jews and all political opponents to the Reich, and were indoctrinated in the SS philosophy of racial superiority.

The recruits were given tuition on weaponry and combat for their guard duties. This involved training on the firing range, marching, and all the basic military necessities that were required to assist the SS. They were not allowed to wear German uniforms or insignia, nor were they allowed to use German armoured vehicles. In the eyes of the SS, all Hiwis were disposable collaborators.

Initially they were supplied with captured Soviet army uniforms, and in the autumn of 1941 they were given the dyed black uniform of the Polish army worn by the former Selbstschütze forces (ethnic-German self-protection units formed after the First World War which operated during the lead-up to the Second World War). In the summer of 1942 they were issued brown Belgian army uniforms for warm weather wear, but frequently wore a mixture of both uniforms. The weapons they were issued with were usually captured enemy weapons, but sometimes they received the standard German infantryman's bolt-action rifle, the Karbiner 98-K. Various other weapons were supplied too as the war progressed.

In 1942 each Wachmänner unit was organised in a squad of fifty men and a platoon of 100–120. These were assigned to companies and battalions under the command of German officers and NCOs.

From the training facility the recruits were now assigned their special tasks. One or two of the companies were stationed in Lublin for security duties, the others were sent to guard labour camps in the Lublin district.

The volunteers were nicknamed 'Trawniki men' or 'Askaries' by the local population. Their duties consisted of supporting the local police units, carrying out deportations, and mass executions of Jews. Their first assignment was to the Belzec death camp where a company-size unit of 100 men was allotted to the camp.

The camp commandant, Christian Wirth, nicknamed 'savage Christian', ruled the camp with an iron fist and encouraged Kapos, Trawniki men and SS personnel to commit terrible acts of brutality against their victims. Wirth had the gas chamber building camouflaged and hidden behind trees with a wire fence around it.

He employed a number of healthy Jews as Sonderkommando to work burying bodies, sorting clothing and valuables, and cleaning the gas chambers. The Trawniki men would be ordered to wait for the new arrivals and then ensure there were no breakouts or panic among the Jews on the ramps. As the train arrived at the ramp, the Sonderkommando helped the deportees get down from the freight cars under the watchful eye of the Kapos, who were often holding truncheons or whips at the ready. The Trawniki men then took up their positions around the reception area and on the surrounding roofs, while another group of armed Trawnikis and SS took up position on the platform. At the unloading ramp the Sonderkommandos took all clothes to a sorting area. They also had to clear the wagons of the deportees who had died en route. Once everyone was removed from the cars they were hosed down with water. The engine driver then shunted the empty carriages out of the camp to make room for the next delivery of cars.

The final stage of the process saw the naked Jews being directed towards the entrance of the gas chamber. Guarding this building stood SS and Trawniki men with dogs. The Trawnikis hurled abuse at the frightened and bewildered men, women and children as they ran by with their hands up, and they beat anyone who showed any sign of reluctance to enter the gas chamber. The so-called 'master of the bath' or Bademeister also shouted to keep the lines moving.

Although their job was horrendous, the Trawniki men considered their posting to a concentration camp comfortable compared to being sent to the Eastern Front to fight with the Wehrmacht. Here they lived in relative ease and were rewarded.

At Treblinka death camp, the Trawnikis supervised the gas chambers and worked the motor that supplied the gas to the gas chamber. Here they had daily contact with the prisoners who worked in the extermination area. Eli Rozenberg, a prisoner working in the extermination area, wrote about a guard named Ivan Marchenko, nicknamed 'Ivan the Terrible': 'This Ukrainian [Trawniki] took special pleasure in harming other people, especially women. He stabbed the women's naked thighs and genitals with a sword before they entered the gas chambers and also raped young women and girls. The ears and noses of old Jews which weren't to his liking he used to cut off. When someone's work wasn't to his satisfaction, he used to beat the poor man with a metal pipe and break his skull. Or he would stab him with his knife. He especially enjoyed entwining people's heads between two strands of barbed wire and then beating the head while it was caught between the wires. As the prisoner squirmed and jumped from the blows, he became strangled between the wires.'

Apart from working in various concentration camps, Trawniki men were assigned to the Reserve Police Battalion 101 to 'cleanse' the ghettos of Jews, sending them to concentration camps. Battalion 101 was a paramilitary formation of the uniformed police force known as Order Police (Ordnungspolizei/Orpo) operating under the command of the SS. Just before operations at Treblinka, Battalion 101 was given the task of deporting Jews from across the Lublin province. Between mid-March and mid-April 1942, 40,000 prisoners of the Lublin Ghetto were loaded by Order Police onto trains destined for Belzec. With the assistance of the Trawnikis from the Sonderdienst Battalion Streibel, an additional 12,000 Jews were deported from ghettos in Piaski, Izbica, Zamosc, and Krasnik.

Not all the inhabitants of the ghettos were sent to concentration, death or labour camps. In Lomazy, as there was no transport, Battalion 101 murdered the men, women and children on the morning of 17 August 1942. Later that day, armed Trawnikis arrived in the main square, where they marched 1,700 ghetto inmates to the Hały Forest outside the town. Jewish men were then forced to dig a trench with an entrance on one side. The Jews were then stripped naked, led in file to the trench, and then the Trawniki began to murder them. A number of the Trawnikis were inebriated from drinking vodka and cognac all afternoon, so policemen from the First, Second and Third Platoons under Lieutenant Hartwig Gnade had to finish the job.

Countless other massacres continued across the General Government with the Trawnikis assisting the Police Battalion 101. There were 2,000 murdered at Parczew, and another 2,000 massacred at the Konskowola hospital.

By the spring of 1943, most towns of the Lublin area were 'free of Jews', but this did not stop the Police Battalion 101 and the Trawnikis going on 'Jew hunts' through the forests, fields and farmlands.

(**Below**) An SS officer identified as Lehnert converses with a woman on the main street of the residential camp in Trawniki. The SS Training Camp Trawniki (Ausbildungslager Trawniki) was both the name of the unit and the facility where its members were trained. The camp was located near the village of Trawniki, 18 miles from Lublin. Established in the Autumn of 1941 under the command of SS-Sturmbannführer Karl Streibel, the training camp produced more than 3,700 guards by the summer of 1943 to serve in the three Operation Reinhard killing centres of Belzec, Sobibor and Treblinka, as well as forced labour camps in the Lublin area, including the Trawniki labour camp, Treblinka I and Poniatowa. Detachments of Trawniki guards were also deployed in the deportation of Jews to the killing centres from ghettos in Poland. Most of the Trawniki guards were recruited from Soviet PoWs. (*USHMM, including caption*)

(**Opposite, above**) View of the Trawniki training camp showing two barracks and a watch tower. Often referred to by their German overseers and Jewish victims as Ukrainians or Latvians and Lithuanians, the Trawniki guards included men of a wide variety of nationalities, including Russians, Belarussians, Poles, Estonians, ethnic Germans, Kazakhs and Tartars. Their training lasted between six weeks and six months and consisted of military drills, weapons instruction, German language training and Nazi ideology. (*USHMM, Staatsanwalt beim Landgericht Hamburg. USHMM caption*)

(**Opposite, below**) Trawniki guards can be seen posing for the camera with a policeman probably in 1942. In the summer the guards were issued with brown Belgian army uniforms, but frequently wore a mixture of the old dyed-black Polish army uniforms as well. They were issued with captured enemy weapons, but sometimes received the standard infantryman's bolt-action rifle, the Karbiner 98-K. Other weapons were supplied as the war progressed.

Group portrait of Trawniki-trained guards at Belzec killing centre in 1942. Relatively few Germans staffed the killing centres and labour camps; most of the work was left to the Trawniki guards. Belzec, Sobibor and Treblinka were run by twenty to forty Germans and guarded by a detachment of 100 to 150 Trawniki.
(USHMM, Instytut Pamieci Narodowej)

Three photographs showing Trawniki men. In 1942 each Trawniki Wachmänner unit was organised in a squad of fifty men and a platoon of 100 to 120. These were assigned to companies and battalions under the command of German officers and NCOs. From training at the Trawniki facility the recruits were assigned tasks. One or two of the companies were stationed mainly in Lublin for security duties, while the others were sent mainly to guard labour camps in the Lublin district.

This photograph, probably taken during a ghetto liquidation in the Lublin district, shows a Trawniki man assisted by an SS NCO knocking a Jewish gentleman to the ground, much to the apparent enjoyment of other Trawnikis.

Trawniki men on bicycles in summer 1943. By this time, apart from guard duties Trawniki men were also assigned to Reserve Police Battalion 101, 'cleansing' the ghettos of Jews and sending them to concentration camps.

Group portrait of members of Police Battalion 101 beneath a sign that reads Krzewie. Members of the battalion participated in the round-up and expulsion of Jews, Poles and gypsies, the guarding and liquidation of ghettos, deportation to concentration camps and the mass shooting of tens of thousands of civilians. The largest massacres were undertaken by Trawniki men. (USHMM, Michael O'Hara)

Two photographs showing the inspection of members of the Reserve Police Battalion 101 by their order police officers in a public square in Lodz. One image is from a photograph album belonging to a member of the battalion. Reserve Police Battalion 101 was a unit of the German Order Police [Ordnungspolizei / Orpo] that during the Nazi occupation of Poland played a central role in the implementation of the Final Solution against the Jewish people and the repression of the Polish population. This battalion carried out a number of operations with the Trawniki men including liquidation of ghettos and massacres. *(USHMM, Michael O'Hara)*

Bernhardt Colberg, a member of Police Battalion 101, in front of their headquarters in the vicinity of Lodz.
(*USHMM, Michael O'Hara*)

(**Opposite**) Two photographs taken in sequence showing members of the Reserve Police Battalion 101 celebrating Christmas in their barracks. On 28 November 1940 the police battalion was deployed to guard the perimeter of the Lodz ghetto. In May 1941 it was sent home to Hamburg, where it was reconstituted: most of its earlier recruits were sent to other police units while new reservists were drafted in. For the next year the new battalion underwent training. Members were given assignments which including guarding and escorting Jewish transports to their final destinations. In June 1942 the battalion was sent back to Poland where it was posted to the Lublin district. For the next few weeks members of the battalion were deployed in rounding-up Jews from smaller settlements and concentrating them in larger ghettos and camps, particularly Izbica and Piaski. (*USHMM, Michael O'Hara*)

Two photographs taken in sequence showing members of Police Battalion 101 engaging in combat training in the vicinity of Lodz. This machine gun was not intended for combat but for policing civilians. It is estimated that between July 1942 and November 1943 Police Battalion 101 was responsible for shooting dead more than 38,000 Jews and deporting 45,000 others. Many of these murders were assisted by Trawniki men. *(USHMM, Michael O'Hara)*

Two members of Police Battalion 101 who are guarding the perimeter of the Lodz ghetto view three Jewish policemen kneeling opposite them on the other side of the fence. (USHMM, Michael O'Hara)

A member of Police Battalion 101 (probably Bernhardt Colberg) poses at the entrance of guard post 5 in the Lodz ghetto. *(USHMM, Michael O'Hara)*

Local residents watch as the Germans publicly hang a woman on a gallows erected in an unidentified Polish town square. The photograph was probably taken by a member of Police Battalion 101. *(USHMM, Michael O'Hara)*

(**Opposite, above**) A Trawniki platoon standing in an open area of Camp I in Sobibor death camp in March 1943. In the background, to the left side, the fire alarm tower from the pre-war era is visible. On the right is the former forester's house which served as living quarters for a few SS as well as being an administrative building. It contained a store room for gold, jewellery and cash collected from victims by the Sonderkommando. (*USHMM*)

(**Opposite, below**) A group of auxiliary Trawniki guards at the Sobibor killing centre, spring 1943. It was taken on the parade ground in front of Camp III. The guard lying in the middle in the front has been inconclusively identified as Ivan Demjanjuk, known at the time as Ivan Marchenko. Indicated in the background are the roofs of two buildings belonging to the murder area. The gable of the barrack in which the Jewish female victims' hair was cut off is visible on the left of the picture. The second roof to the right of it, with a higher chimney-like structure, belonged to the building with the gas chambers. (*USHMM*)

(**Above**) A group photo of a Trawniki platoon at the Sobibor killing centre, spring 1943. This photo was taken on the parade ground in front of Sobibor Camps II and III. The second guard from the left back row may be Ivan Demjanjuk. Demjanjuk was transferred to Sobibor on 26 March 1943 together with eighty-two other Trawniki men. The guards badges of rank are clearly visible in the group photograph. While epaulets without stripes mark ordinary guards; one, two and three stripes in ascending order correspond to the ranks of senior, group, and platoon guards. Demjanjuk, 'Ivan the Terrible', was sentenced to death in 1988 for war crimes, but the sentence was later overturned. (*USHMM*)

SS-Oberscharführer Siegfried Graetschus (second from right) in the Spring of 1943 with four Trawniki men, more than likely on the parade ground between Sobibor II and III. Siegfried Graetschus was responsible for training the Trawniki men at Sobibor. (*USHMM*)

In the middle of the photograph is SS-Hauptscharführer Johann Niemann who is standing between two Zugwachmänner (train guards) in front of one of the Trawniki housing barracks in Sobibor in spring 1943. Alexander Kaiser, a Trawniki man, is most likely on the right with an adjutant cord on his uniform tunic. Niemann was deputy commandant and directly perpetrated the murder of thousands of Jews in the camp. In mid-1943 there were reports of a possible revolt within the camp. Niemann ordered seventy-two Jews to be executed to quell any intentions that the prisoners might have had of trying to escape. A few months later, on 14 October 1943, a prisoner uprising did take place. Niemann was the highest-ranking SS officer on duty that day, and was killed in the tailor's barracks with an axe to the head by Alexander Shubayev, a Jewish Red Army soldier imprisoned at Sobibor. Shubayev escaped and joined a partisan group but was killed. (*USHMM*)

Three Trawniki train guards and four Gruppenwachmänner stand next to a guard building in the entrance area of Sobibor in spring 1943. (USHMM)

Trawniki men march in formation at the Sobibor death camp in spring 1943. (USSHM)

SS-Scharführer Paul Groth (centre) and Trawniki men stand in front of an elaborately carved sign 'Abprotzstelle', a sign post to the toilets in Sobibor. (*USHMM*)

A group of Trawniki men appear to be erecting a fence and are in the process of piling the wooden pillar into the ground. (*USHMM*)

(**Above**) Trawniki men in front of one of the Trawniki housing barracks in Sobibor. Alexander Kaiser is in the front on the right. Probably as a joke, someone in the barracks holds an alarm clock up to the window. *(USHMM)*

(**Opposite**) Two photographs in sequence showing Trawniki and SS personnel marching in the Płaszów labour camp. These men were used as guards to supplement the German SS staff until the official redesignation of Płaszów as a concentration camp in January 1944. Thereafter the camp was staffed by 600 men of the SS Totenkopfverbände (Death's Head Units). *(USHMM, Leopold Page Photographic Collection)*

(**Above**) A photograph taken during the liquidation of the Warsaw Ghetto uprising in April 1943. Armed Trawniki men can be seen in a doorway observing a group of dead Jews. Forces embroiled in the uprising fighting included 2,000 well-armed troops including Waffen-SS Panzergrenadier troops, Wehrmacht anti-tank battery, and a battalion of Ukrainian Trawnikimänner. Ukrainian, Lithuanian and Latvian auxiliary policemen known as Askaris (Latvian Arajs Kommando and Lithuanian Saugumas), and technical emergency corps were to join the task force to combat the uprising. (NARA)

(**Opposite, above**) Trawniki men with SS soldiers during the clearing operation of the Warsaw uprising in May 1943. Supported by regular SS soldiers, the Trawniki were ordered to round up the remaining Jews and either march them out of the ghetto or load them onto trucks.

(**Opposite, below**) Trawniki men from Treblinka pose for the camera.

Chapter Five

Last Years

By the late summer of 1943, nothing could hide the fact that the German war machine was suffering a military catastrophe on the Eastern Front. As a result the SS began the process of decommissioning the concentration camps. The remaining Jewish prisoners, and the Sonderkommandos and Kapos, were told that if they worked well they would be treated fairly.

One problem the Nazis had always had was body disposal. The task of exhuming hundreds of thousands of corpses from the burial pits was a logistical nightmare. For this gruesome task the Sonderkommandos (prisoners under the supervision of the Kapos) and Trawniki men, were set to work to remove the corpses and burn them either in the functioning crematoria or on pyres. Once this process had been completed, which often took weeks, the camps would be closed down.

The average Sonderkommando working in the killing facilities was only supposed to work for three months. According to SS policy they would then be gassed and replaced by new arrivals to ensure secrecy. Some survived for a year or more because they possessed specialist skills, but they always had the worry that they may one day be taken away from their duties and murdered. It is believed that from the conception of a death camp to its liquidation, on average there were some fourteen generations of Sonderkommando that worked and died there. With the prospect of the camps being closed down the prisoners and Sonderkommandos feared for their lives even more.

At Treblinka the inmates planned a revolt. Monday, 2 August 1943, was chosen because Monday was a regular day of respite from gassing. When a group of SS personnel and forty Trawnikis drove off to the River Bug to swim, the conspirators, including Sonderkommandos, ran riot for thirty minutes, setting buildings ablaze. A group of armed Jews attacked the main gate, others attempted to climb the fence. However, SS machine-gunners and armed Trawniki guards slaughtered most before they had a chance to break out.

With rumours spreading about sites being decommissioned there was increasing unrest among the surviving prisoners and the Sonderkommando. On 14 October 1943, members of the Sobibor underground, led by Soviet-Jewish PoW Alexander Pechersky, masterminded an uprising in the Sobibor death camp. They managed to kill eleven SS officers, overpower the Trawniki guards, and seize weaponry. Although the plan was to kill all the SS and walk out of the main gate of the camp, the killings were discovered and the inmates ran for their lives under a hail of fire. Some 300 out of the 600 Sonderkommandos escaped into the forests, but most were recaptured by search squads and executed.

Several months later at Auschwitz-Birkenau there was unrest among the Sonderkommando. In the previous year the number of Sonderkommando working at the camp had risen from 300 to 900, due to the Hungarian intake. The Sonderkommando were working round the clock in the four crematoria supervised only by a handful of SS men. At the end of June 1944, owing to the increased workload, the Sonderkommando were moved from Barracks No. 13 in Section BIId to live in Crematoria II, III and IV. Among the prisoners were nineteen Soviet PoWs from Majdanek who incited members of the Sonderkommando to revolt. A group of Sonderkommando leaders then began planning an uprising. The plans did not come to fruition until news reached them that Auschwitz was soon to be decommissioned. On 7 October the insurgents carried out a number of attacks including setting Crematorium IV on fire, causing serious damage, and then attacked SS personnel alerted by the flames and smoke. In the confusion that ensued a number of inmates managed to cut through the fence and escape outside. However, their success was short-lived and the SS together with Trawniki men managed to pursue them, surround them, and kill them. About 250 Jews died fighting, including leaders Załmen Gradowski and Józef Deresiński. The SS lost three killed and ten wounded. Later, four Jewish women who had stolen explosives from the nearby Union-Werke armaments factory and supplied it to the Sonderkommando conspirators were hanged in public. Of those who did not die in the uprising, 200 were later forced to strip and lie face down before being shot in the back of the head. A total of 451, half the workforce of the Sonderkommandos, were killed on this day.

In January 1945 at Birkenau, the Sonderkommandos dismantled all the killing apparatus, and the incineration ditches were cleared and levelled by them with the help of physically able prisoners. They then emptied the pits which had been filled with the ash and crushed bones of murdered prisoners and covered them with fresh turf. On the night of 17 January, 58,000 prisoners were evacuated from Monowitz and Auschwitz.

On 20 January the crematoria were blown up, apart from Crematorium IV which had been demolished after it had been damaged by fire following the Sonderkommando revolt. Then special SS units murdered around 700 prisoners including most of the Sonderkommandos. As for the Kapos, they were instructed along with the Trawnikis to assist in the evacuation of the inmates from the camp and sub-camps.

Nazi officers standing in front of a building in Solahutte, the SS retreat outside Auschwitz. Karl Hocker is third from the right. Far right is SS-Obersturmführer Max Sell (Arbeitseinsatzführer in Auschwitz and afterwards in Mittelbau-Dora). Also pictured in the back centre is Hermann Baltasar Buch. From 1943 until September 1944 Buch was in charge of Crematorium IV in Birkenau and oversaw the Sonderkommandos there. (USHMM)

Three SS officers dine in Auschwitz: Dr Eduard Wirths is seated in the centre, Höss is on the right, Vinzenz Schoettl is on the left. (USHMM, Peter Wirths)

Six photographs showing Jewish women and children from Subcarpathian Rus awaiting selection on the ramp at Auschwitz-Birkenau. Sonderkommandos assisted the newly arrived transports. (*USHMM, Yad Vashem*)

Elderly Subcarpathian Rus Jews resting from what was probably an arduous journey to Auschwitz. These people would probably have been murdered within a couple of hours of their arrival at the camp. (*Auschwitz-Birkenau Museum*)

(**Above**) SS guards supervising the arrival of a transport of Jews from Subcarpathian Rus to Auschwitz-Birkenau in May 1944. Far right is SS Wachmann Stefan Baretzki. Often selection was carried out with two columns being divided into four columns: two of women and children, and two of men. Those unfit for labour were sent towards the crematoria, while all able-bodied workers were interned in Auschwitz, or were retained ready at a moment's notice to be transferred to other camps in the Reich. The selection for labour in each transport varied daily, sometimes it was as low as 10 per cent, sometimes 50 per cent, but most Jews that arrived through the gates of Birkenau in May 1944 were immediately sent to their death. Roughly 3,300 people arrived per day, sometimes up to 4,300. On 20 May, for instance, one convoy arrived with 3,000 people, of whom some 1,000 were able, and 2,000 were unable to work. The following day on 21 May two convoys were reported to have arrived from Hungary with 6,000 people of whom 2,000 were able to work and the remainder were sent directly to their deaths. During that day both the incinerators of Crematoria II and III were being serviced so the victims were disposed of in the three incineration ditches next to Crematorium V. Though the specially built track from the crematorium to the pits had been laid it was never used because it was considered an inconvenience. Instead the Sonderkommando had to drag the corpses from the gas chamber to the pits. (*Auschwitz-Birkenau Museum*)

(**Opposite & following**) A series of images showing prisoners in the Aufräumungskommando (cleaning commando) sorting through personal belongings confiscated from Jews arriving from Subcarpathian Rus in May 1944. Some 1,500 prisoners worked in the 'Kanada' in two shifts sorting through plundered Jewish possessions. The Kanada was a treasure trove to the members of the SS who benefitted from the wealth. Diamonds, gold, coins, dollars, foreign currency from all over Europe were stolen. Food and alcohol too were taken for personal use or sold. Clothing and furniture were taken by the SS as well. The Auschwitz authorities deemed that all valuables from the new arrivals were the property of the Nazi state, and that individual profit was a crime. (*Auschwitz-Birkenau Museum*)

Four SS officers gather for drinks in a hunting lodge. From left to right are Franz Xaver Kraus, Karl Moeckel and Commandant Richard Baer. Kraus was brought to Auschwitz in December 1944 to manage the evacuation of the camp. Himmler had sent out an order that all the personal effects from the warehouses at Auschwitz, as well as building material and equipment, were to be transported back to the Reich. Half of the 150,000 prisoners held captive in Auschwitz, most of them Poles and Russians, were to be moved to concentration camps in the west. (USHMM)

View of one of the destroyed crematoria at Auschwitz-Birkenau immediately after the liberation. In late 1944 the Sonderkommando were ordered to dismantle all the killing apparatus at Auschwitz. The incineration ditches were cleared and levelled, and pits which had been filled with the ash and crushed bones of murdered prisoners were emptied and covered with fresh turf and plants. At Birkenau, Crematoria I, II, III and IV were dismantled and usable parts transported to other camps. (USHMM, Mark Chrzanowski)

(**Opposite, above**) Women in the barracks of the newly liberated Auschwitz concentration camp. (*NARA*)

(**Opposite, below**) A shipment of bedding, partially covered with snow, lies strewn next to an abandoned train in Auschwitz-Birkenau immediately after liberation. (*USHMM, Mark Chrzanowski*)

(**Above**) View through the barbed wire fence of the burning Kanada barracks in Auschwitz-Birkenau immediately after the liberation. Original caption: '"Kanada" burns. Before leaving, the Germans set fire to magazines and piles of prisoner's clothing.' (*USHMM, Mark Chrzanowski*)

(**Opposite, above**) A group of female survivors of Auschwitz-Birkenau trudge through the snow as they depart from the camp through the main gate. Original caption: 'A group of Frenchwomen on their way to freedom. They have already shed their prison uniforms and put on clothes taken from burning magazines. Main gate is on the right.' (*USHMM, Mark Chrzanowski*)

(**Opposite, below**) Corpses of Auschwitz prisoners in Block 11 of the main camp (Auschwitz I), as discovered by Soviet war crimes investigators. (*USHMM, Instytut Pamieci Narodowej*)

(**Above**) Auschwitz Commandant Rudolf Höss is guarded by American and Polish soldiers before his transfer to Poland where he will stand trial. Höss was executed on 16 April 1947. He never regretted creating Auschwitz and developing it into a mass killing centre. His only regret, as he walked up the wooden steps to the gallows, was that the Nazis had lost the war. (*USHMM, Eddie Murphy (estate)*)

(**Opposite**) A Russian soldier examines the roof hatch where Zyklon B crystals were poured into the gas chamber at Majdanek death camp. An SS man tasked with the gassing procedure would climb onto the roof protected by a gasmask and throw in the saturated Zyklon B pellets. They waited twenty-five minutes until the screams fell silent, then the doors and windows were opened and the Sonderkommando went in to remove the corpses for disposal.

(**Above**) Moses Korn, a Jewish prisoner forced to work in Sonderkommando 1005, poses next to a bone-crushing machine in the Janowska concentration camp. This photograph was taken soon after liberation for the Extraordinary Commission or the Red Army. The Sonderkommando 1005 units were officially called Leichenkommando (corpse units) and inmates were often put in chains to prevent escape. Sonderkommando 1005 were assigned to remove all traces of the 'final solution of the Jewish problem' by Einsatzgruppen and all other executions including murders in various concentration camps. The bone-crushing machine operated from autumn 1942 to autumn 1944.
(*USHMM, Belarusian State Archive of Documentary Film and Photography*)

(**Opposite, above**) View of a wagon piled high with corpses outside the crematoria in the Buchenwald concentration camp. This photograph was taken after the liberation of the camp by Lieutenant Colonel Parke O. Yingst of the US Army. Its apparent that concentration camp personnel never had the time to incinerate these corpses. (*USHMM, Patricia A. Yingst*)

(**Opposite, below**) Former concentration camp inmates search through clothing and other effects after the liberation of Buchenwald. This photograph was taken by Dr William Garrison Birch who served with the 45th Evacuation Hospital as a US Army medical officer. (*USHMM, Stephen Jacobs*)

(**Above**) Former SS guards from Buchenwald who have been captured by American troops march along a street with their hands behind their heads. (*USHMM, Harvey S. Heaton*)

Starving prisoners are liberated at Woebbelin concentration camp. Original Caption: 'At the German concentration camp in Wobbelin, many inmates were dying of starvation when troops of the U.S. Ninth Army captured the camp. Here an inmate thinks he has been forgotten when some have been removed to hospitals, but he will leave as soon as the worst cases have gone. 82nd Airborne Div., Wobblin, Germany. 5/4/45.' (USHMM, Laszlo Berkowits)

Corpses lie strewn about the Buchenwald concentration camp following liberation.
(USHMM, Claranne Bechtler)

Partial view of the crematorium, focusing on the chimney, in the newly liberated Dachau concentration camp. The photograph was taken by Alexander Zabin, who was an American soldier with the 4th Auxiliary Surgical Group in the US Third Army, when he visited Dachau in mid-May 1945.
(USHMM, Colonel Alexander Zabin)

(**Opposite, above**) Group portrait of survivors standing next to the moat in the Dachau concentration camp following liberation. (USHMM, Peggy McClure)

(**Opposite, below**) Survivors in Dachau rebuke an SS guard captured by US troops while in the background American soldiers summarily execute other camp guards. (NARA)

(**Above**) American soldiers of the 42nd Rainbow division capture fleeing SS men near Dachau concentration camp. (NARA)

Captured SS guards in the newly liberated Dora-Mittelbau concentration camp. *(USHMM, Francine Feeney)*

Camp guards killed in revenge killings lie next to a wall in the Dachau concentration camp. US Army soldier Paul Richard Averitt took this photograph. It was on 29 April 1945, only hours after its liberation, that his unit arrived at Dachau concentration camp and witnessed the horrific scenes which he captured on film. *(USHMM, Angie Averitt Womack)*

Notes

Notes

Notes

Notes

Notes

Notes

Notes

Notes

Notes

Notes

Notes

Notes

Notes

Notes